Britain's Best Bakeries

written and photographed by
Milly Kenny-Ryder

Thank you to my three boys – Simon, Wilf and Zephy – for all your pastry-related patience. Gabriel, thank you for your expert photo editing and Jo, for your multi-faceted assistance. And to Jennifer Earle and Edd Kimber for your advice on brilliant bakeries.

Britain's Best Bakeries
First edition, first printing

Published in 2024 by Hoxton Mini Press, London
Copyright © Hoxton Mini Press 2024. All rights reserved.

Text and photography by Milly Kenny-Ryder*
Front cover illustration by Sean Thomas
Editing by Florence Ward
Series design by Hoxton Mini Press
Production design by Richard Mason
Proofreading by Zoë Jellicoe

*Except for following images: p.2: Chatsworth Bakehouse © Ed Schofield; p.4-5: © Laura Edwards; p.8-9: © Adriana Giakoumis; Pophams (first, third and fourth images) © Adriana Giakoumis, (second image) © Gabriel Kenny-Ryder; Chatsworth Bakehouse (first image and third image) © Ed Schofield; E5 (first image) © Rachael Smith, (second image) © Helen Cathcart; Eric's (first image) © Anton Rodriguez; Panadera Matthew © SJ Weller; The Dusty Knuckle (second image) © The Dusty Knuckle; Jolene (third image) © Philippa Langley; Cédric Grolet at The Berkeley (all images) © The Berkeley; St. John © Harriet Langford; The Connaught (first and last images) © The Connaught; Violet Cakes (second and last images) © Oliver Hooson; Oast (first image) © Joe and Charlotte (@joeandcharlotte); The Exploding Bakery © Sam Harris; Landrace (all images) © Gabriel Kenny-Ryder; Rye © Gabriel Kenny-Ryder; Sol © Ed Schofield; Nova © Sarah Lemanski; Pollen (first image) © India Hobson; Aran (last image) © Kimberley Grant / Rural Studio; Bandit © Peter Leonard; Two Eight Seven © Flora Mansen; Twelve Triangles © Murray Orr; p.224 (first image) © Gabriel Kenny-Ryder.

A CIP catalogue record for this book is available from the British Library. The right of Milly Kenny-Ryder to be identified as the creator of this Work has been asserted under the Copyright, Designs and Patents Act 1988.

ISBN: 978-1-914314-64-3

Printed and bound by Livonia Print, Latvia

Hoxton Mini Press is an environmentally conscious publisher, committed to offsetting our carbon footprint. This book is 100 per cent carbon compensated, with offset purchased from the printer's offsetting scheme.

Every time you order from our website, we plant a tree:
www.hoxtonminipress.com

FSC
www.fsc.org

MIX
Paper | Supporting
responsible forestry
FSC® C002795

Previous page: Toad (p.92)
This page: Fortitude (p.54)

Above: Farro (p.156)
Opposite: Long Boi's Bakehouse (p.186)

Pophams (p.20)

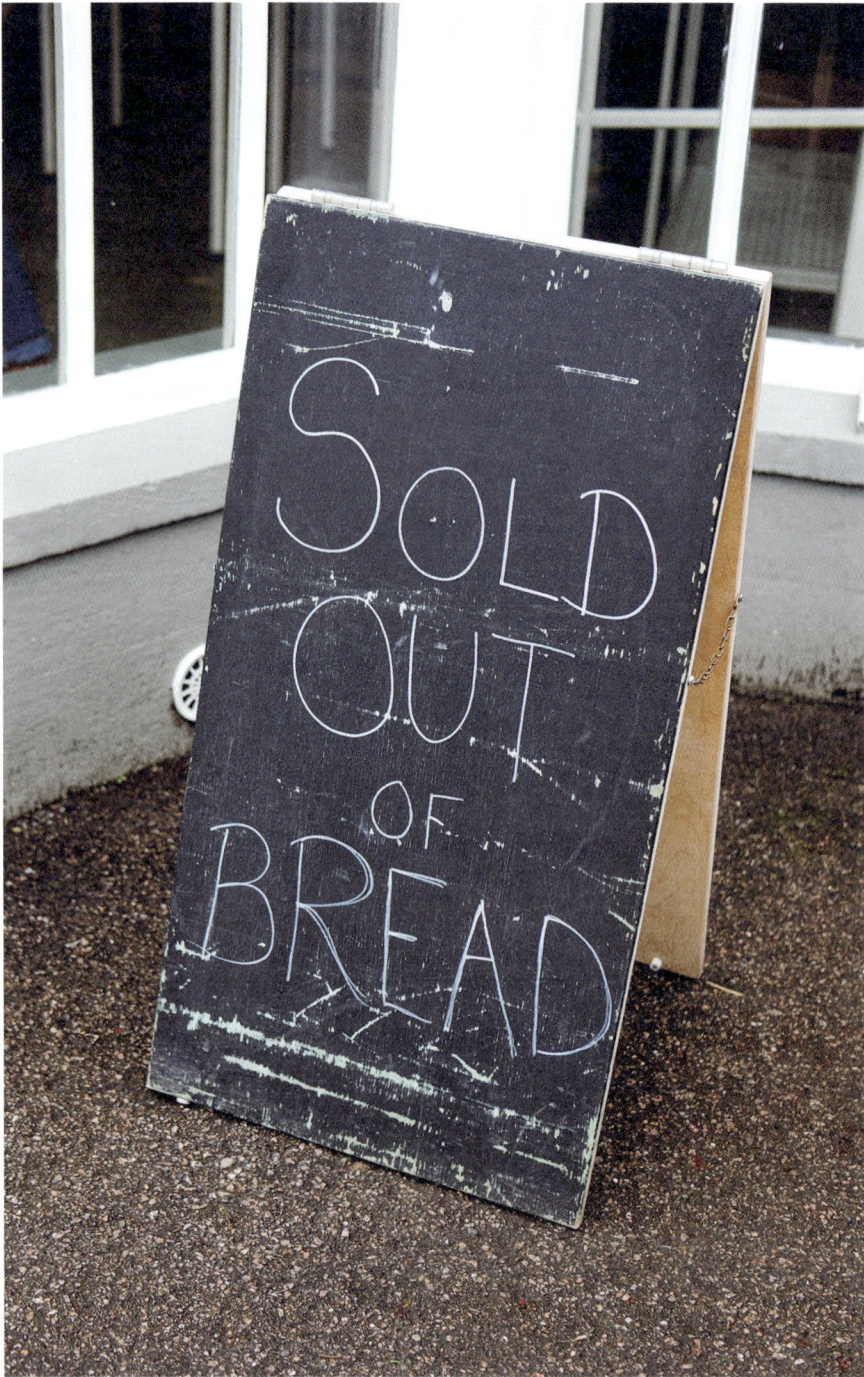

Contents

The Best For...

BREAD   For the upper crust of artisan baking, sample Triangle's (p.184) ultra-nutritious and gut-friendly loaves made with heritage grains like rye, spelt and einkorn, or a pillowy slice of Hamblin (p.110) sourdough made with wheat grown within 50 miles of the bakery.

PASTRIES   Head to Lannan (p.220) for a pain Suisse that is (almost) too beautiful to eat, Arôme (p.32) for viennoisserie with an Asian twist (with added ingredients like nori, coconut and miso) or Companio (p.194) for decadent fillings like chocolate ganache or spiced pumpkin crema. But if you're a croissant purist, nothing beats Farro's (p.156) perfectly flaky classic.

CAKES   Like your cakes immaculately constructed and shaped like flowers, nuts or even dogs? Book a spot at The Berkeley (p.68) or The Connaught (p.88) for afternoon tea. Prefer a slice of good old-fashioned tray bake, sprinkles and all? Head to Violet (p.98), where the cakes come with a seal of royal approval.

SANDWICHES   The focaccia sandwich reigns supreme. The Dusty Knuckle (p.50) load theirs with plenty of spiced veggies, cheese, yoghurt and chilli, Sol (p.166) give the English classics an Argentine upgrade (enter the Argie BLT: smoked beef, lettuce, tomato and chimichurri mayo) and, if you're organised enough to pre-order online, Chatsworth Bakehouse (p.24) push the limits of how many delicious fillings you can fit between two pieces of bread.

PIZZA   Forno's (p.62) Roman-style pizzas are loaded with Italian goodies like stracciatella, salame rosa and mortadella, or Toklas's (p.96) 'strecci' tops a thin focaccia base with rotating seasonal produce.

BRUNCH	It's not all grab and go: take your time at The Old Store (p.146) with plenty of comfy seating and brunch classics like croque monsieur or pancakes; head to Pollen's (p.190) roomy Ancoats site for a slice of sourdough topped with smoked salmon or roasted wild mushrooms; or while away a morning sitting in the window at Glasgow's Outlier (p.216) with an impossibly indulgent beef shin cheese toastie.
SOMETHING UNUSUAL	Head to Toad (p.92) for croissants topped with jalapeños or filled with slow-cooked ham and pineapple relish. For a sweet tooth, try Margot's (p.102) tangy sourdough babka or Long Boi's (p.186) cute Fairy Bread Bostock (brioche toast, strawberry jam, frangipane and sprinkles).
WITH KIDS	The play area at Rye (p.168) is the perfect place for little ones to run off a sugar high, or Miel's (p.76) child-friendly workshops will inspire the next generation of bakers.
FILLING STORE CUPBOARDS	E5's (p.28) shelves are stacked high with artisan goods, including British cheese, bean-to-bar chocolate and a brilliant selection of cookbooks. Grain Culture's (p.142) Bake Shop General Store is a treasure trove of tasty things to try, from local honey to craft beers.
BAKING WITH A CAUSE	Kitty and Al from Orange (p.116) are championing the positive impact that baking can have on mental health, sharing Kitty's own moving story and raising money for charity, while Proof Social Bakehouse (p.124) and E5's (p.28) Poplar branch offer paid training and employment to marginalised groups including prison leavers and members of the refugee community.
LOCATION	Enjoy a peaceful canalside coffee and cake at Rye by the Water (p.82) and watch the ducks and kayaks glide by, or head to Layla (p.72) to fuel up on flaky pastries before mooching around buzzy Portobello Market.

The rise of the artisan bakery

My love of bakeries comes from growing up in a big French family. Long, hot summers were spent in Provence, where boulangerie shelves were stacked with baguettes and pastries baked that morning, warm and buttery, handed over in a brown paper bag. A fresh pain au chocolat, the ultimate reward, was often offered as a tradeoff for traipsing along to an early-morning antiques market with my grandparents. My addiction has continued to grow ever since.

People in Britain have been baking bread for thousands of years, and recipes for pastry even appear in medieval recipe books. But for a long time, viennoisserie – breakfast pastries like croissants, Danishes and pains au chocolat – was the domain of mainland Europe. Most of the bread sold in Britain was heavily processed, mass-produced, plastic-wrapped and picked up in supermarket chains.

All of this has changed over the last decade, and it has been remarkable to witness the rise of independent bakeries across the country, with artisan (handmade, additive-free) bread and viennoisserie at the helm of the new offerings. Being trapped in our homes during the global pandemic seems to have reignited a passion for wholesome food products and practices. Worldwide, people found comfort in the simple act of nursing a sourdough starter and baking the perfect banana bread. There is something therapeutic about making your own sustenance; nourishing our bodies with good quality bread and pastries feels like a small but precious necessity.

This is part of a bigger growing interest in slower lifestyles, with more attention to craftsmanship, growing your own food, home fermenting and shopping for ultra-local British ingredients from independent producers. Pubs and alcohol consumption are on the decline, while bakery and coffee shop culture continues to soar. Social media is only fuelling the trend, with elaborate pastries and loaves produced as art objects regularly going viral. There is a communal investment in the bakery boom, with many recent start-ups such as Tarn (p.40) and Quince (p.80) asking communities to support Crowdfunder campaigns, so we are all attached to a cause before it has even opened its doors.

It was a near impossible task whittling my exhaustive research list down to just 62 bakeries – in truth there are many, many more worth visiting. Britain boasts a brilliantly diverse range of bakeries serving everything from traditional Jewish challah and St Lucian cornbread to Turkish pide, plus a plethora of teashops offering delicate sponges and scones. Many of these baking traditions have been thriving here for generations, but they aren't the main focus of this book. My love for baked goods started in French boulangeries, and the bakeries I've chosen here are mostly born from this tradition, championing buttery laminated pastries and artisan bread this side of the channel.

So how did I decide what to include? Mainly, I was looking for somewhere worth a detour, to steal the Michelin Guide's line. The bakeries included in this book are noteworthy for their ethical practices and imaginative flavours – see Toklas (p.96), with its Bourbon peach melba Danish, or Toad's (p.92) unexpectedly delicious beef rendang croissant. Some drench their goods in butter; others, like plant-based Bandit (p.204), eschew it altogether.

The location can be unexpected. There are bakeries on industrial estates, within five-star luxury hotels and everything in between. Some have popped up as a response to Covid, while others, like Kossoffs (p.64), have been in the family for generations. Some operate as a grab-and-go takeaway service; others invite you to slow down, grab a newspaper and sit for a while. Some have growing teams and multiple branches, but many are run by just a baker or two. Whatever the size of their operation, they are all friendly and welcoming, imparting genuine passion for their craft.

I feel like I have been researching this project long before it actually began as a 'real' writing and photographic assignment. The excuse to finally call my pilgrimages to new bakeries 'work' has been very useful when it comes to my long-suffering family and friends, who regularly stand in rainy queues with me pre-9am. I hope you will deem this selection of venues worthy of your time queuing and waiting. Making a humble croissant or loaf of sourdough is a lengthy process; it only seems fair that we give a little of our time to receive our tasty reward.

Everyone has their favourite bakery, and I feel the need to apologise in advance to anyone who feels offended that their most-loved isn't featured in these pages. I've become immune to people professing their love for one bakery or another, stating that it 'must be included' – but I can't pretend I wasn't swayed when my favourite bakers confided in me about their go-to places, and I'm excited to be sharing some of these hidden gems with you.

Milly Kenny-Ryder
London, 2024

The language of baking

Wheat: a grass that is cultivated for its seed (grain), which is then ground to make flour. White flour is made from only one part of the grain, stripping away the fibrous outer shell and nutrient-rich core. Wholewheat flour uses the entire grain.

Rye: rye is another grass and part of the wheat family, but rye grain has a different gluten composition to wheat, resulting in a denser, chewier texture.

Spelt: spelt is an ancient species of wheat that has been grown since around 5000bce, said to be more nutritious than modern grains. Spelt is lighter and slightly sweeter than wholewheat flour.

Buckwheat: buckwheat is neither a wheat nor a grain – it comes from the seeds of a plant distantly related to rhubarb. It is a nutrient-rich and fibrous alternative to gluten with a nutty, slightly bitter flavour.

Einkorn: the oldest species of wheat known to scientists, einkorn is naturally low-gluten and easy to digest. It has a deep, nutty flavour.

Heritage grain: a term referring to any variety of wheat, rye, barley or oats grown before the intensive plant breeding of the twentieth century. They are richer in nutrients than modern, processed grains.

Stoneground or stone-milled flour: any wholegrain flour produced via the traditional process of grinding grains between two millstones.

THE DOUGHS

Leavened dough: dough containing yeast or another leavening agent (like baking powder) that will cause it to rise. The yeast converts sugars and starches into CO_2, which is then trapped as air pockets in the dough – a process known as fermentation. Unleavened dough, e.g. flatbreads, do not rise because they don't contain a leavening agent.

Sourdough: a naturally leavened bread, meaning that it relies on a mixture of wild yeast and good bacteria (a 'starter') to rise, rather than on commercial yeast.

Slow-fermenting: an ancient bread-making process whereby the bread mixture ferments for a longer period (anywhere between four hours and several days) before it is baked. The resulting bread is lighter and fluffier.

Enriched dough: any dough made with ingredients other than flour, water and salt. Enriched doughs may include eggs, oil, butter or sugar and are softer and richer than doughs made without.

Laminated dough: many thin layers of dough separated by butter, which gives the dough a flaky texture. Puff pastry and croissants are both examples of laminated dough.

THE BREADS AND BUNS

Brioche: bread enriched with eggs, milk and butter, giving it a very soft texture and rich, sweet flavour.

Babka: a Jewish braided bread, made from an enriched dough that is rolled out, spread with a topping like chocolate, rolled, sliced into strips, braided and then baked in a loaf tin.

Shokupan: also known as milk bread, this Japanese bread uses a yudane – a paste of flour and boiling water – which is mixed into the dough, adding more liquid to the dough than is possible in a traditional recipe and resulting in a very soft, fluffy loaf.

Focaccia: a flat, leavened Italian bread made from a base similar to pizza dough. The dough is flavoured with olive oil and can be topped with herbs and vegetables.

Challah: an Ashkenazi Jewish braided bread made from a dough enriched with eggs.

Fougasse: similar to focaccia, fougasse is a French flatbread, traditionally shaped into a wheat sheaf.

Cinnamon bun: originally from Sweden, a bread bun made from an enriched dough that is rolled out, topped with cinnamon, rolled up, sliced and left to rise again.

Bostock: created as a way to use up stale brioche, a bostock is a slice of brioche drenched in syrup, topped with jam, almond paste and nuts, then baked again.

THE PASTRIES AND CAKES

Viennoisserie: baked goods made from yeast-leavened dough that is often laminated with plenty of butter. Viennoisserie is typically associated with France but they actually originated in Austria: the term – French for 'things from Vienna' – was first used to describe the goods sold by an Austrian baker who opened his Boulangerie Viennoise in Paris in the 1830s.

Patisserie: unlike viennoisserie, patisserie is not made with leavened dough. Patisseries such as eclairs or macarons are normally baked first, then decorated by pastry chefs.

Croissant: a laminated pastry made from yeast-leavened dough that is rolled out and layered with butter multiple times, resulting in a flaky texture.

Pain au chocolat: a French pastry made from croissant dough filled with chocolate batons.

Pain Suisse: a French pastry made from croissant dough filled with vanilla cream and chocolate chips.

Danish: a laminated pastry made from a yeast-leavened dough, often topped with custard or fruit. Unlike croissants, Danish pastry dough contains eggs, needed to create a studier dough that can hold fillings.

Bear claw: a spin on the Danish originating in the USA, the bear claw is Danish pastry dough filled with a sweet almond filling.

Cruffin: a hybrid croissant/muffin, the cruffin is made by baking laminated croissant dough in a muffin mould.

Canelé: a small, cylindrical French pastry with a caramelised crust and custard centre normally flavoured with vanilla and rum.

Pastel de nata: a Portuguese puff pastry tart filled with egg custard.

Maritozzi: an Italian delicacy, made up of an enriched dough bun filled with whipped cream.

Sfogliatelle: an Italian pastry, consisting of numerous layers of thin, flaky pastry filled with ricotta, semolina and lemon zest.

Empanada: a Spanish or Latin American pastry filled with savoury ingredients and then baked or fried.

Galette: a French word describing any kind of flat, free-form cake, often resembling a fruit tart with the crust folded part-way over the filling.

Madeleine: a small French sponge cake with a distinctive shell shape.

Kouign-amann: though the name means 'butter cake' in Breton, this is technically a pastry made with laminated dough, resulting in a texture that is slightly denser than a croissant.

Lamington: an Australian cake made from squares of sponge coated in chocolate and then rolled in coconut.

Pophams

Pastries, pasta and pretty homeware

Heralded as one of London's first speciality bakeries, Pophams has rightfully gained cult status in the capital. Founder Ollie Gold (with business partner Lucy McWhirter) opened a tiny spot in the backstreets of Islington in April 2017, taking over a derelict chemist and giving it a DIY transformation (they even had to learn plumbing and tiling). They've expanded since then, adding a further two branches in east London. Their bacon and maple Danish, made with thick streaky rashers and a generous lick of syrup, has been on the menu since day one and this sticky, salty treat is still a favourite with regulars (always ask for it warmed). The London Fields location also operates as a restaurant, with generous sandwiches and soups at lunchtime and homemade pasta in the evenings. And if gorging on their pastries isn't enough, pop into their chic homeware store (they have shops next door to the Islington and London Fields branches) to pick up handmade ceramics, vintage embroidered tea towels and other gifts to emulate the bakery's vibe in your home.

19 Prebend Street, London N1 8PF
Other locations: London Fields, Victoria Park
pophamsbakery.com

Chatsworth Bakehouse

London's most popular sandwiches

It may be easier to get a Glastonbury ticket than to bag one of Chatsworth Bakehouse's hefty sandwich of the week, but this tiny red bakery is worth visiting even if you haven't pre-booked a sarnie. Chef Tom and his partner Sian started the venture during lockdown as a creative way of supplying those in need with comforting, bready sustenance while using up produce that would have otherwise been wasted. Sian masterminds the operation behind the scenes while Tom and the team handmake every element of their celebrated sandwiches in the affectionately named 'Phonebox'. The Anerley Hot sandwich is a particular favourite – fennel salami, Neapolitan salami, prosciutto crudo, chilli pepper spread, roasted garlic aioli, sharp provolone, pickled fennel, bitter leaves and hot honey dressing, stacked on their freshly baked focaccia – but if you miss out during the week, you can buy slabs of their hearty focaccia pizza at the weekend.

120a Anerley Road, London SE19 2AN

chatsworthbakehouse.com

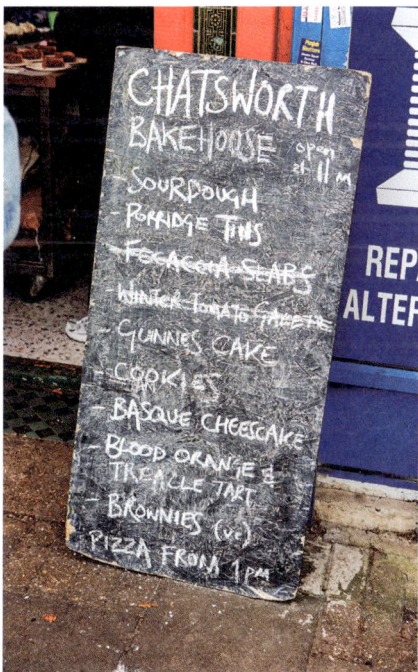

CHATSWORTH
BAKEHOUSE open
at 11 am
- SOURDOUGH
- PORRIDGE TINS
- FOCACCIA SLABS
- WINTER TOMATO GALETTE
- GUINNESS CAKE
- COOKIES
- BASQUE CHEESCAKE
- BLOOD ORANGE &
TREACLE TART
- BROWNIES (ve)
PIZZA FROM 1pm

E5 Bakehouse

Field-to-table baking under Hackney arches

E5 is led by a vision of what they call the 'Agrarian Renaissance': decentralising our food system by working with small-scale farmers using sustainable techniques that keep the planet healthy. So you can feel good about eating this bread, which is made with flour milled on site from grain grown on their farm in Suffolk. The good doesn't stop there: in 2017, E5 opened a Poplar Bakehouse where they employ and train people from refugee communities, investing profits back into projects that support and welcome refugees arriving in the UK. But it's the Hackney branch, found under the railway arches of London Fields overground station, that has a special, wholeheartedly local feel. A jolly and (at times) chaotic place to spend your Saturday morning, come here to feast on an organic brunch, stock up on bread or natter with a friend over good coffee and pastries.

396 Mentmore Terrace, London E8 3PH
Other location: Poplar
e5bakehouse.com

RAILROAD

THE PERFECT LOAF
THE PERFECT LOAF
THE PERFECT LOAF

SOURDOUGH
PANETTONE and
VIENNOISERIE

DAY BAKING

DOLCE

RIAZ PHILLIPS EAST WINDS
RIAZ PHILLIPS EAST WINDS
RIAZ PHILLIPS EAST WINDS
RIAZ PHILLIPS EAST WINDS
RIAZ PHILLIPS EAST WINDS

babas
bites

Soil to table

DON'T
SWITCH

Arôme Bakery

French viennoisserie with an Asian influence

Arôme's menu is a gloriously creative blend of French viennoisserie and pan-Asian flavours. The founders, Singaporean restaurateur Ellen Chew and French Pâtissier Alix André, are unafraid to experiment with the classics, and the results are staggeringly beautiful and delicious, from miso bacon escargot – a perfect umami hit for anyone craving a salty, savoury snack – to the signature Arôme Honey Butter Toast (a thick slice of fluffy shokupan with a crunchy caramelised honey crust). Other inventive highlights include a smoky gula melaka coconut bun and a laksa tomato roll, topped with fresh coriander. With a space designed by Taiwanese artist and architect Rain Wu, Arôme is minimalist and airy, each detail meticulously considered from the warm woodwork to the satisfying, systematic organisation of the counter. Items will sell out thanks to the constant arrival of hungry fans, but don't worry: everything on offer is incredible.

9 Mercer Street, London WC2H 9QJ
Other location: Marylebone
instagram.com/aromebakerylondon

27 Duke Street

W1U 1LE

London

Eric's

Queue-worthy sweet treats

Helen Evans, much-celebrated former head baker of Flor (now closed), is the powerhouse behind south London's new kid on the block. This neighbourhood spot was highly anticipated prior to opening thanks to Helen's illustrious CV, and the hype hasn't died down yet. Fair warning: you'll be standing in a queue long enough to form lasting friendships with those in front of you – but it's worth the wait. Come early and enjoy chatting to fellow fans about what you are going to order when your time at the till arrives. Helen champions UK-grown wheat, particularly from no- or low-impact farming systems like The Fresh Flour Company in Totnes and Hodmedod's in Suffolk. There are always new things to try on the tempting chalkboard menu, but Eric's cinnamon buns are wondrously soft (thanks to the brioche-style enriched dough) and their mini almond croissants are ideal for littler visitors.

20 Upland Road, London SE22 9EF

ericslondon.com

Tarn Bakery

A bakery with a view

Pastry addicts will know Florin Grama as the discerning but humble baker who worked magic behind the scenes at Pophams (p.20) and Flor. Now he's teamed up with friend and fellow chef Felix Ortona Coles (they met working at Michelin-starred St Barts in Smithfield), the duo bringing a wealth of expertise and passion. Tarn's sourdough bread uses UK-grown grains, and their pastries include classic croissants and pains au chocolat, plus more unusual sweet and savoury bakes, such as apple and whey custard or gorgonzola and squash Danishes. Tarn opened quietly at the end of 2023 and has a charming neighbourhood feel, surrounded by other friendly community businesses, at the top of a steep hill with impressive city views. It's a small space with just a few seats to perch at, so better treated as a takeaway – which is perfect, given that the Parkland Walk and Highgate Wood are on the doorstep.

83 Hazellville Road, London N19 3NB
*instagram.com/tarnbakery_*

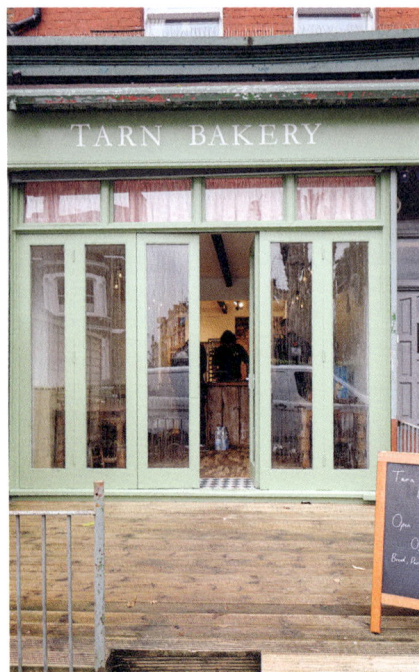

TARN BAKERY

Panadera

Fan favourite Filipino bakery

'Panadera' translates as 'female baker' in Tagalog, and this dinky bakery found a stone's throw from Camden Town was named to honour the Filipino mothers who pass culinary traditions down to their children. Founders Florence Mae Maglanoc and Omar Shah are also the dream team behind the smash-hit ice cream parlour Mamasons – just down the road from the bakery – so they know a thing or two about creating crowd-puller. Many make the pilgrimage here to try their loaded sandwiches, made with pandesal (a Filipino milk bread similar to shokupan) and filled with corned beef hash, panko chicken or mushroom, but their sweet goods are just as impressive. Try the doughnuts topped with cubes of leche flan (the Filipino answer to crème caramel), a slice of vibrant ube (purple yam) tart or a super fluffy, dangerously moreish pan de coco bun (just 60p each), and then wash it all down with a matcha latte or malty Milo mocha.

83 Kentish Town Road, London NW1 8NY
panaderabakery.com

Cut the Mustard

Hidden gem with hefty pastries

You'll spot Cut the Mustard from afar, the retro yellow logo popping against the pared-back black exterior of both branches. It may be a little removed from London's primary bakery circuit, but it's worth making the trip to Tooting to sample some of the more unusual bakes on offer here. If you have the appetite, try the Chocolate Hazelnut Dream, a satisfying weighty cross between a pain au chocolat and a twice-cooked hazelnut croissant, filled with chocolate batons and nutty paste – but their plain croissants are just as tasty. If the pastries have sold out, opt for a flavoursome black pudding sausage roll or an indulgent brownie. It's also worth getting your hands on a 'Frank' sourdough – charmingly named after owner Jimmy's grandfather – which is a blend of organic white and wholemeal flour, naturally fermented for 22 hours.

180 Franciscan Road, London SW17 8HG
Other location: Moyser Road
cutthemustardcafe.com

The Dusty Knuckle

Pizza and sandwiches for a good cause

The Dusty Knuckle is a Dalston institution. Set up by three friends in 2014, the bakery radiates positive spirit and genuine passion through every inch of its 40-foot shipping container home. A self-described 'purpose-driven business', the Dusty Knuckle is a social enterprise that offers training, mentorships and employment to young people who need it the most. The Dalston site is sheltered, with plenty of seats outside (plus a handful of indoor tables for chillier days). Come for al fresco pizza in the warmer months – or head to the cosier Harringay branch, where you can order pizza at the weekend all year round. They're best known for their giant focaccia sandwiches (filled with mouthwatering combinations like marinated paneer, curried tomato sauce, mint yoghurt, pickled carrot salad, dried coconut, crispy garlic and chilli drizzle), but everything here is delicious. If you are looking to improve your skills, they also offer baking and cooking classes – a great gift for foodies.

Abbot Street Carpark, London E8 3DP
Other location: Harringay
thedustyknuckle.com

Fortitude Bakehouse

Fun pastries with a Moroccan twist

You'll probably spot the queue before the bakery when it comes to Fortitude. Tucked away on a cobbled mews in Bloomsbury, this bustling bakehouse has been a staple on the London food scene since it opened in 2018. Dee Rettali opened Fortitude with partner Jorge Fernandez (who previously ran the successful Fernandez and Wells cafes in Soho), aiming to exclusively use either sourdough starters or fermented batters for both bread and cakes, giving the flavour an extra dimension and richer taste. With roots in Morocco, Dee's flavours are often inspired by north African cuisine: harissa chicken hand pies, Berber omelette batbout (pita), merguez chermoula rolls and bear claws infused with orange water, served alongside coffee or Tangier tea. The team are astonishingly productive, instantly restocking empty trays with batches of freshly baked pastries. There is something here to satisfy any craving, from savoury puff pastries to cookies with decadent soft serve in summer months.

35 Colonnade, London WC1N 1JD
fortitudebakehouse.com

ALMOND
&
ORANGE
BEAR CLAW

APPLE
&
CUSTARD
HAND
PIE

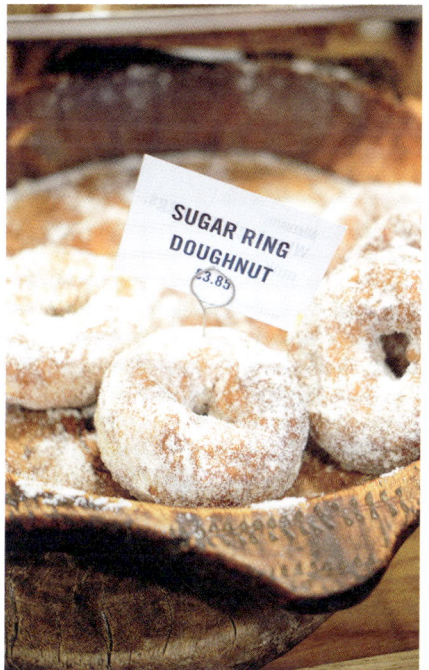

SUGAR RING
DOUGHNUT
£3.85

Jolene

London favourite on a roll

That the Jolene sites seem to multiply across London every season is testament to the quality of their bakes and the charm of their venues. The original branch opened on Newington Green in September 2018, the third eatery from restaurateur Jeremie Comettoo-Lingenheim and chef David Gingell (of Primeur and Westerns Laundry fame). The burnt terracotta facade, with its logo designed by the graphic designer's six-year-old, is very east London, but there is substance as well as style here. The kitchen and bakery make everything from crusty bread to glossy pastries on site, which makes you feel very much part of the action, delicious scents wafting round the chatter-filled dining room. Dinner here is a feast of creative flavours, but their seasonal cookies and cakes are perhaps the most memorable: generously iced spiced pumpkin loaves, double chocolate sea salt cookies and wedges of raspberry and vanilla sponge so perfect you can't imagine biting into them.

324 Hornsey Road, London N7 7HE
Other locations: Shoreditch, Stoke Newington
bigjobakery.com

PAIN AU CHOCOLAT 380

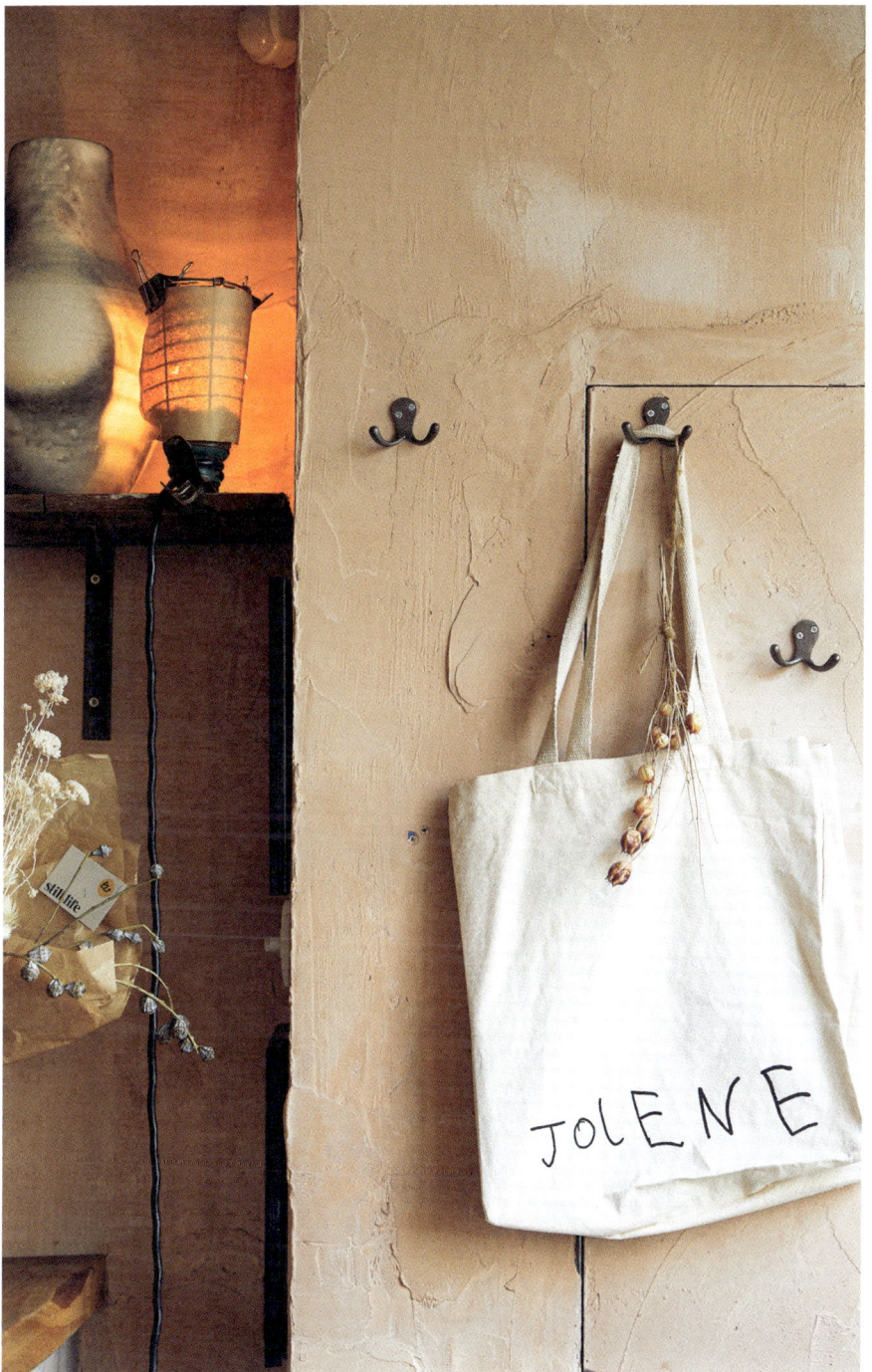

Forno

Italian treats in the heart of Hackney

This bakery, deli and pastificio from Mitshel Ibrahim – the founder and head chef of nearby pasta restaurant Ombra – is characteristically Hackney, with worn brick walls and a minimalist industrial look inside. But their offering is decidedly Italian, from Roman-style pizzas (with toppings like rocket pesto, parma ham, heritage tomatoes and stracciatella) to the iconic, elegant maritozzi (a mini brioche bun filled to the brim with ethereal white whipped cream) – usually the first thing to sell out. If you are lucky, you may also spy their shell-shaped sfogliatelle dusted in icing sugar, an Italian delicacy that's not easy to find done well in London. Forno is well-placed for a walk along Regent's Canal after securing your snacks, but if you're sticking around then browse the small shop for homemade pastas and sauces, or even treat yourself to a glass of wine at one of their inside tables.

322 Andrews Road, London E8 4RP
forno.london

ESPRESSO	2.8	CIABATTA	2 - 3.5
MACCHIATO	3	SOURDOUGH	2.5 - 5
AMERICANO	3	SEEDED	4 - 6
FLAT WHITE	3.5		
LATTE	3.5	MARGHERITA	6
CAPPUCCINO	3.5	PIZZA OF THE DAY	7 - 9
HOT CHOCOLATE	3.5		
TEA	2.5		
WINE			
JUICES			

Kossoffs

A bakery with 100 years of history

The story of this north London institution began in the 1920s when Wolf Kossoff, a Jewish refugee from Kyiv, established the first Kossoffs Bakery in London's Arnold Circus. The business continued to grow as two generations took Kossoffs across London in the 1980s, with the aim of bringing locals traditional Jewish baked goods. Years after the family business had closed, Kossoffs Kentish Town opened in 2021, with Aaron Kossoff (Wolf's great grandson) and his girlfriend Jo Clarke at the helm. The couple met working at Little Bread Pedlar and together transformed Aaron's father's closed North London site into a beautiful, modern bakery and cafe. They've expanded from the Jewish classics, the counter now heaving with viennoisserie – their pain au chocolat is the bestseller, but the triple-baked almond croissant is also legendary. Kossoffs champion UK dairy and flour producers and serve coffee from Saint Espresso, who created a Kossoffs blend especially for them.

259 Kentish Town Road, London NW5 2JT

kossoffs.com

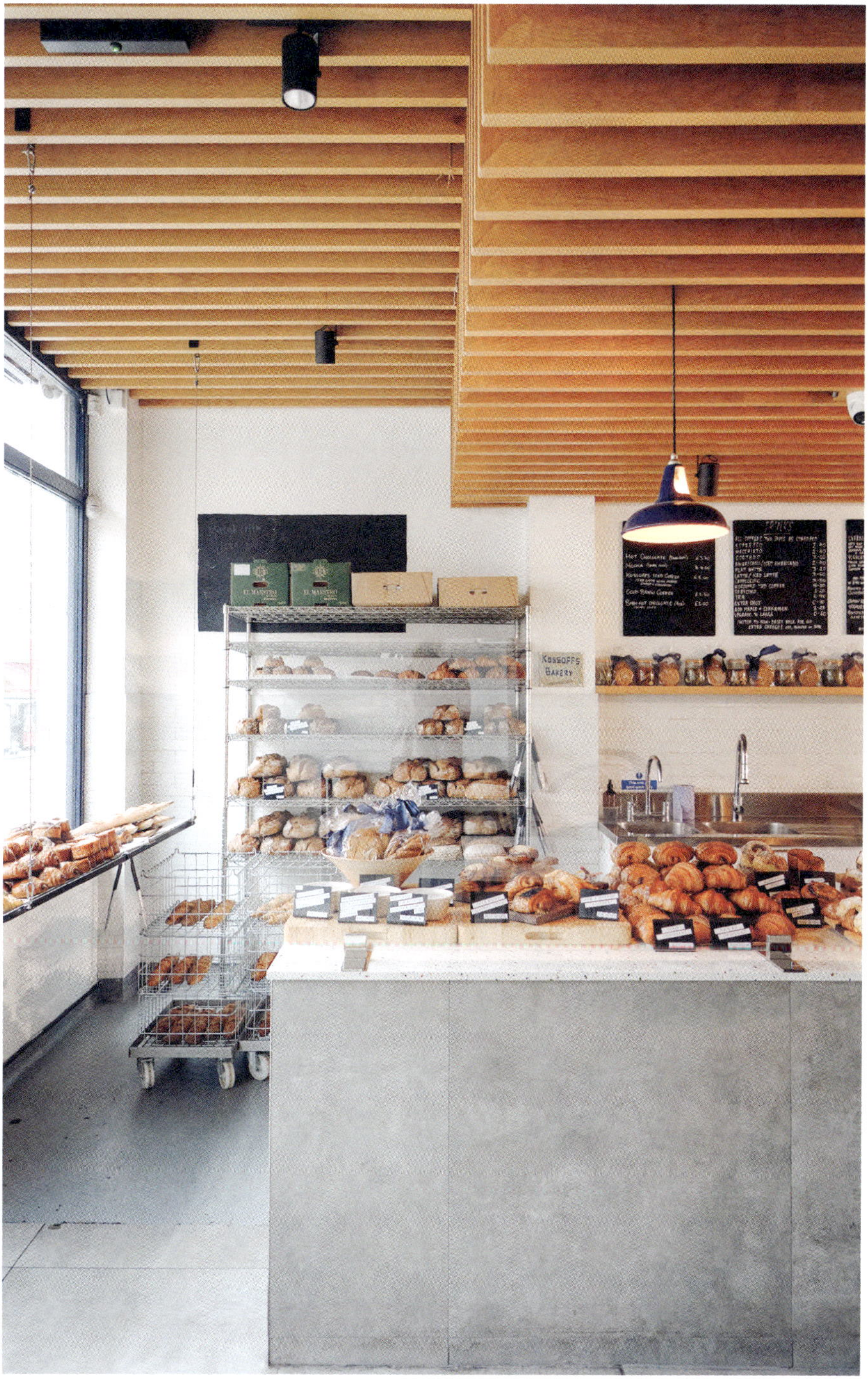
EL MAESTRO
EL MAESTRO
KOSSOFFS
BAKERY

Cédric Grolet at The Berkeley

Renowned chef's first patisserie outside Paris

Cédric Grolet's cakes and patisserie are so immaculate that they often look like illusions. The French chef made a name for himself heading up the pastry department at five-star hotel Le Meurice in Paris before opening several stand-alone venues in the city. He then won World's Best Pastry Chef in 2018, causing a sensation on social media – so it's no surprise that his first international site, at The Berkeley Hotel in London, opened to great fanfare in early 2022. Grolet is best known for his fruit, flower and nut creations, found alongside a stunning breakfast menu of viennoiserie (his multi-layered pain Suisse is particularly impressive). Pop by to pick up pastries to scoff in nearby Hyde Park, or book a spot at the chef's counter for a tasting menu of the kitchen's 'PastryLab' creations. The hotel also serves afternoon 'Goutea' (a fusion of 'le goûter', French for children's snack time, and British afternoon tea) including masterpieces like the truffle egg croissant and vanilla flower patisserie.

Wilton Place, London SW1X 7RL
the-berkeley.co.uk/restaurants-bars/cedric-grolet-at-the-berkeley

Layla

Bringing artisan baking to west London

When lockdown sent the world into a sourdough-baking frenzy, Tessa Faulkner went one step further. Inspired by the pandemic to start her own bakery, the doors to Layla opened in 2021. It was immediately in good company, joining the independent businesses of the Golborne Road area in Notting Hill, a neighbourhood awash with creative restaurants and queue-worthy cafes. But even here, Layla stands out. The interior design is minimalist, but the bakes are endlessly creative: juniper and lime swirls, chocolate barley bows, truffle Tunworth pain Suisse, all imagined by Head Baker Colton Dinner (who previously worked at the celebrated Ledbury restaurant). There are also unusual breads to satisfy your tastebuds, from seeded spelt, honey and lovage to delicately bitter nettle focaccia. The Layla devotees are a stylish crowd, but everyone here is delightfully friendly and there is a feeling of palpable excitement as each customer reaches the counter.

332 Portobello Road, London W10 5SA
laylabakery.com

SODA BREAD 5.5
PAIN SUISSE

Miel

Bakes with a classic French influence

It is difficult to say whether it's the tasty bakes or the cheerful team that are more persuasive when it comes to Miel Bakery. Their quaint, dusty blue facade stands out next to blander businesses on Warren Street. Owner-chef Shaheen Peerbhai has a background in classic French cookery at Michelin-starred establishments, bringing an obvious French influence to her counter of patisserie and pastries. She crafts the viennoisserie using flour milled traditionally in Normandy, Valrhona chocolate and butter from Poitou Charentes (for those not in the know, they make the best butter in France). Miel's striped hazelnut gianduja croissant is reliably delicious, and the caramelised kouign-amann (a sweet Breton cake made from laminated dough) is also a winner. If you're left feeling inspired, book onto one of Shaheen's intimate baking workshops, which take place inside the bakery.

60-61 Warren St, London W1T 5NU
mielbakery.co.uk

Quince Bakery

Championing the finest British fruit

The quince may be an out-of-fashion British fruit, but Anna Higham's debut bakery is firmly on trend, opening to much anticipation in February 2024. Championing traditional baking techniques and British fruit, Anna's baked creations often showcase the eponymous quince (golden, aromatic and somewhat pear-like), like the quince and rice pudding tart or her roast pork sandwiches with quince aioli. From floating shelves to an open-plan layout allowing customers to see every stage of the process, the bakery's design is meticulously imagined and executed. Her bakes are seasonal and ingredient-driven, but you won't find viennoisserie here. Instead, Quince focuses on bread (made with Britain's best stoneground flour) and hand pies (a kind of pasty made using vibrant seasonal fruit, such as rhubarb, apricots and peaches) – and of course, the signature brown butter buns that made Anna famous when she worked at Flor.

267 New North Road, London N1 7AA
quincebakery.co.uk

Rye by the Water

Canalside community hub

Hidden away in an unlikely corner of residential developments among the Brentford canals, Rye by the Water feels like a culinary anomaly in the area – which makes it all the more special. The waterside cafe is an idyllic spot for weekend breakfasts, and an especially great pitstop for cyclists riding along the river in need of a buttery reward. Chef Robin Gill, who already has several celebrated restaurants under his belt (including Sorella and Bottle & Rye in south London), opened Rye by the Water in summer 2019, with Aisling Chaudhuri taking the reins as head chef. Their signature loaf is a naturally leavened sourdough with a tangy flavour and a satisfyingly bouncy texture. But there's more to this bakery than their bread: Chaudhuri teams up with visiting chefs for a series of supper clubs, while the outdoor terrace is used for summer residencies, most notably the Ruben's Reubens BBQ partnership.

Catherine Wheel Road, Brentford TW8 8BD
ryebythewater.com

St. John Bakery

Iconic doughnuts

You've probably heard of St. John, every foodie's favourite producer of hearty nose-to-tail cooking, but what about St. John's bakeries? Here, you'll find less offal and more icing sugar, but each of the three locations shares the characteristically unfussy style of Fergus Henderson's food empire, white-walled and industrially lit with food as the focus. St. John's signatures are their famously plump, sugary doughnuts, filled with raspberry jam, vanilla or chocolate custard (or, occasionally, some kind of seasonal deviation – the slightly sour, slightly sweet rhubarb and apple jam was a good one). The St. John clan have impeccable taste, so it's worth picking up a bottle of wine or a pot of homemade granola from their shelves to bring a bit of magic to your store cupboards at home.

72 Druid Street, London SE1 2HQ
Other locations: Covent Garden, Borough
stjohnrestaurant.com/a/restaurants/bakery-arch

St. JOHN

VANILLA
DOUGHNUT
£2.80

INGREDIENTS
Wheat Flour, Milk, Egg, Sugar, Yeast, Salt, Butter

St. JOHN

RASPBERRY JAM
DOUGHNUT
£2.80

INGREDIENTS
Wheat Flour, Sugar, Raspberry, Water, Butter, Egg,
Salt, Yeast, Butter

The Connaught Patisserie

Immaculate cakes and chocolate dogs

The Connaught may be a grand dame hotel in the heart of swanky Mayfair, but it's worth making the trip here to sample the achingly beautiful creations of Master Pâtissier Nicolas Rouzaud. Decked out in blush pink, from the flag marking the entrance to the carpets, walls, chairs, lights and even the takeaway coffee cups, every corner and crumb of this pastry mecca is delicate, considered and sweet. The chocolate Connaughty Hound – a chocolate, hazelnut and praline cake so precisely textured that it even gives the impression of having fur – is a mainstay; other seasonal beauties might include a jewel-like pistachio and strawberry tart or a gold-flecked cashew Paris-Brest. There are tourists, of course, but it is also a popular spot for those living and working nearby, a special place to meet and mull over business with a rhubarb and raspberry brioche and coffee. Everything here is so exemplary, made and presented with the utmost care and attention to detail, that even the most basic of baked goods (like a classic baguette) feel like the day's ultimate treat.

16 Carlos Place, London W1K 2AL
the-connaught.co.uk/restaurants-bars/the-connaught-
patisserie-by-nicolas-rouzaud

Toad Bakery

Unusual savoury creations

Toad was once Frog, but an unfortunate name clash with a bold restaurateur meant the name change was essential to avoid a lawsuit. This brand diversion has only encouraged more love for the Camberwell bakery, which many claim to be London's finest. Toad was opened in 2022 by Rebecca Spaven and Oliver Costello, who previously fine-tuned their craft working at Ottolenghi and Fortitude Bakehouse (p.54). It's a tiny, unfussy takeaway spot with only filter coffee on offer, but the goods – from a savoury croissant stuffed with pork belly, red cabbage and cheddar to a sweet yuzu, orange and almond Jaffa Cake – are seriously delicious. And the team are delightfully unserious (visit on Valentine's Day and you might be handed a condom to go with your heart-shaped baguette). One thing's for sure, you'll walk away from Toad will a smile on your face and a (very) full belly.

44 Peckham Road, London SE5 8PX
toadbakery.com

Toklas

Creative pastries and pizza

What do Toklas bakery and Frieze have in common? Both founded by art world titans Amanda Sharp and Matthew Slotover, this smart, concrete space is (appropriately) filled with just as much striking artwork as it is striking bakes. Set in a 1970s brutalist building in Temple alongside its sister restaurant of the same name, Toklas's offerings are simple, classy and beautiful. Breads, patisserie and pastries are all created by Head Baker Janine Edwards and her team, and quality produce is at the heart of the offering, with the evolving Danishes using English fruit and cream (a recent winner balanced Bourbon-poached peaches atop crème diplomat and tangy raspberry coulis, sprinkled with flaked almonds). At lunchtime, the slices of 'strecci' come out: super thin squares of pizza with delectable toppings like courgettes and olive tapenade or potato and nduja.

9 Surrey Street, London WC2R 2ND
toklaslondon.com/toklas-bakery

Violet Cakes

Royalty-approved cakes

Violet has been a favourite on the east London scene for years, but it reached a wider audience after owner Claire Ptak was summoned to bake the royal wedding cake for Meghan and Harry. Claire started out selling from a stall on Broadway Market but opened her Californian-style bakery (with whitewashed walls and a sunny disposition) in 2010. Everything is made using all organic or low-intervention ingredients and seasonal options pop up throughout the year, but the favourites never leave the menu. The vegan California cake, a white-iced square topped with sprinkles, is a slice of childhood traybake nostalgia, and you can't go wrong with a perfectly piped American-style cupcake (made grown-up with flavours like chocolate with bergamot). Violet's egg yolk cookie is also iconic – the recipe omits egg white, using just the yolk to create a more indulgent cookie with a squishy centre.

47 Wilton Way, London E8 3ED
violetcakes.com

- Cheddar green onion toastie
- Blue cheese kimchi toastie
- Quiche
  - with salad leaves

boiled egg 2.⁰⁰ . ½ Avo 3.⁰⁰ . leaves

12

Margot Bakery

The best babka in London

Michelle Eshkeri opened the much-loved Margot in 2016. The offering is astonishingly wide (and whole-heartedly delicious), from traditional Jewish breads (her challah and babka are unrivalled) to classic French-style almond croissants, pains au chocolat and seasonal Danishes. Michelle's use of sourdough starters is especially creative, from sourdough babka to sourdough bagels (sold on 'bagel day', a monthly triumph that sees even the local rabbi stop by to get his fix). The small cafe is a pretty place to while away a morning, with several benches for enjoying a leisurely coffee and bite to eat as sunshine streams in over the patterned tiled floor. The supply dwindles throughout the day as many of the regulars come for their weekly hit, so get there early to avoid disappointment.

121 East End Road, London N2 0SZ
margotbakery.co.uk

Grain and Hearth

Microbakery turned seaside hotspot

Whitstable is a lovely weekend destination, just big enough for small adventures and with plenty of quaint allure. You're spoilt for choice when it comes to oysters and fish and chips, but for breakfast there is only one place you should seek out. Grain and Hearth was set up by Adam and Carmen Pagor in 2019 after the success of their home-based London microbakery. It is a cosy venue with worn wooden tables and moody lighting specialising in sourdough bread, which is fermented overnight, allowing the sour punchy flavour to develop more. Don't overlook their majestic croissant loaf, made using unsold pastries from the previous day. Start your weekend here, stocking up on supplies from their abundant shop of speciality food items.

Rear Store, 50-52 Oxford Street,
Whitstable, Kent CT5 1DG
Other location: Faversham
grainandhearth.co.uk

Gwyn's Bakery

Nut-free pastries and breads

A gem of the West Sussex food scene, this Horsham bakery is owned by Ben Lines, whose extensive cheffing experience includes a stint at triple-Michelin-starred The Fat Duck. Humble in every sense of the word, Ben chose to honour his mother's great uncle with the bakery's name. The purpose-built building is refreshingly spacious, an open-plan bakery and cafe, with clean stylish design by Jon May. Gwyn's core range includes a variety of sourdough, white and wholegrain loaves, and the pastry section highlights the team's nut- and sesame-free kitchen with linseed chocolate croissants and seasonal Danishes. But from the sweet pastries, it is the pillowy sugar encrusted cinnamon buns that are a favourite with regular customers, with their addictive balance of sugar and spice. Order a takeaway coffee (made from ethically sourced beans that are roasted locally, of course) and appreciate the brilliantly cheerful illustrated paper cups by Tom's friend, Joanna Hu.

26 Bishopric, Horsham RH12 1QN

gwynsbakery.co.uk

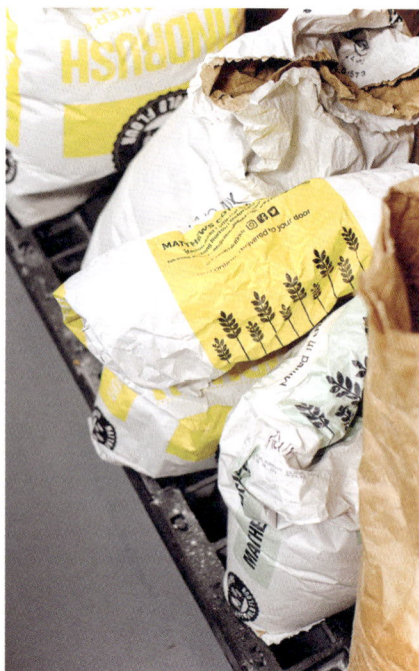

Hamblin Bread

Oxford's star bread business

Wander east from Oxford's dreaming spires and Hamblin is found on the city's edgier, artier outskirts in a flurry of shops and cafes that is also home to the great Missing Bean coffee roasters. Opened in 2018 by Hugo Thurston and Kate Hamblin, the bread here is made using stone-ground flour from organic wheat and rye, all grown within 50 miles of the bakery. Their sourdough, with a robust flavoursome crust but soft and pillowy inside, is the perfect vehicle for a generous dollop of butter. The star of the show may be bread, but there are sweet and savoury options to satisfy any craving, from hearty sausage rolls and pizzas to addictive cinnamon buns and melt-in-the-mouth chocolate cookies. Get to Hamblin too late and you'll be met at the door with a sad signpost announcing that the goods are sold out. Luckily for anyone who treasures their lie-in, you can order the day's treats online and pick them up before 1pm.

247 Iffley Road, Oxford OX4 1SJ
hamblinbread.co.uk

Modern Provider

Delicate bakes in delightfully kitsch cafe

Margate prides itself on producing and promoting exciting and unique independent businesses, and Modern Provider is just that. A refreshing antidote to the proliferation of pared-back bakery interiors, this eccentric venue is a museum of curiosities, the walls plastered with vintage adverts for hot dogs or 7 Up and the shelves populated with kitsch trinkets. Owner Ben Wykes left a job at Burberry to follow his dream to live by the sea, and Modern Provider delivers British seaside charm in spades. The retro memorabilia is delightfully tacky but their bakes are high-end – the pain Suisse in particular is a thing of beauty, flaky dough folded over an oozing centre of pastry cream and chocolate, dusted with icing sugar. As well as feeding hungry locals and tourists, Modern Provider bakes bread for neighbouring businesses including Turner Contemporary and The Falstaff in nearby Ramsgate.

4-5 The Centre, Margate CT9 1JG
instagram.com/modern_provider

BREAD CAKES
&
PASTRIES
7up
ICE CREAM

Softa-freez
HOT DOGS

M Modern Provider
MILK EGGS
&
PROVISIONS

Orange Bakery

A family business with plenty of heart

It's easy to adore the father-daughter team behind Orange, who radiate kindness and enthusiasm for everything they do. Al taught his daughter Kitty to bake as a coping mechanism when she suffered from depression, and their shared hobby bloomed into a small business. At one point sleeping next to the oven as it was the only place where she felt safe, Kitty's love and passion for bread have grown ever since, and she now helps others find the joy in baking with her creative initiatives – most recently the Kitty's Kits bread mixes. Each item on the menu has a story, from the Albert loaf, a tribute to Kitty's brother who prefers white sliced to sourdough (delicious toasted with butter and marmite), to the brilliantly creative half-pizza half-bagel 'bialys' (halfway between a pizza and a bagel). Not only are the Orange Bakery team talented; they're promoting a great cause – 100 per cent of the Kitty's Kits profits go to Breaducation charity, which gives free bread classes and kits to schools, prisons, food banks and community groups.

Watlington Town Hall, High Street,
Watlington, Oxfordshire OX49 5PY
theorangebakery.org

Pinch

Home of the cruller

The cronut was born in NYC in 2013 and hybrid pastries have multiplied ever since, with the dangel, brookies and cruffins all featuring on fad cafe menus. These Frankenstein creations can become gimmicky in other hands, but not so with Pinch's crullers. These elegant circular donuts are made from deep-fried choux pastry, the name hailing from the early 19th-century Dutch word 'krullen' (to curl). As tasty as they are photogenic, owner Alice's quirky cruller flavours include apple cider and candied walnut; honey and bacon; and coffee and hazelnut. It's not easy to find Pinch, discreetly signposted down a farm track road in rural Suffolk, and the bakery inside is very much a working site. Perch on a colourful stool to watch Alice piping, frying and icing the crullers (a mesmerising process) and indulge in one of the many other sweet treats available while you wait.

East Green, Kelsale, Saxmundham,
Suffolk IP17 2PJ
eatpinch.com

Proof Social Bakehouse

Social-enterprise bakery with excellent vegan options

Combining Head Baker Paul Dickinson's ten years' of experience with a worthwhile mission, Proof is the brainchild of the Tap Social Movement – a social enterprise that offers paid training and employment to prisoners and prison leavers. Found within Oxford's Sandford Lane Industrial Estate, the open-plan cafe offers an immersive view of the working bakery, the scent of baking filling the cavernous space. Their fruit Danishes are bestsellers, but Proof also cater generously for vegans with an impressive spread of dairy-free options (it's unusual to find a vegan almond croissant as good as theirs). If you fancy a hot drink, the baristas pour a great flat white with Oxford's best-loved Missing Bean coffee, while the pantry area sells a range of artisan items from the bakery's favourite suppliers.

68 Sandford Lane Industrial Estate,
Kennington, Oxford OX1 5RP
proofbakehouse.com

Pump Street Bakery

Renowned chocolatiers (and equally talented bakers)

The dusty-pink facade of this pioneering specialty bakery has become almost as iconic as the sweet creations they sell inside. Pump Street Bakery was one of the first destination artisan bakeries in the UK and are well known for their craft chocolate, made by hand from bean-to-bar using traditional methods. Located in a 15th-century building on the charming Suffolk coast, the bakery was founded in November 2010 by father and daughter team, Chris and Joanna Brennan. You'll find their chocolate at their boutique across the road, but it's worth sampling a pain au chocolat with your coffee so you can taste it in action, enveloped in addictively flaky pastry. But this isn't all they're known for: pick up other Pump Street favourites from the generously stocked counter, including the bear claw (croissant dough folded over a light almond frangipane, finished with a dusting of icing sugar) or their excellently humble Eccles cake (butter puff pastry punctuated with currants and raisins).

1 Pump Street, Orford, Woodbridge IP12 2LZ
pumpstreetchocolate.com/pages/our-locations

Staple Stores

Serving up pastry staples by the sea

The Kent coast is home to a cluster of newly opened independent restaurants, boutique hotels, appealing shops, galleries and (of course) tempting bakeries. Staple Stores is indeed a staple in the area, the original Broadstairs branch such a success that owners Stephen Gadd and Rachel Young have now opened sites in Westgate and Ramsgate. The small, stylish cafes are minimalist, with pared-back decor and a clean, chic Instagram page to match (their popular custard slices, showcased as perfect, squidgy cross-sections, are iconic on the grid). The larger Westgate store also serves hot food, oozing cheese toasties, focaccia sandwiches and comforting quiches – all of which are made in house. It's an ideal breakfast pitstop before a bracing walk on the beach.

19 St Mildreds Walk, Westgate-on-Sea CT8 8FZ
Other locations: Broadstairs, Margate, Ramsgate
staplestores.co.uk

HOT   COLD

Oast

Trendy neighbourhood spot

This lovable neighbourhood bakery is found in Margate's hippest district, Cliftonville. Run by husband-and-wife team Will and Charlotte, Oast is named after the buildings synonymous with the Kent countryside (the area's Oast Houses, with their signature conical roofs, were traditionally used to dry out hops). It is a calming space, with muted dark green tones and communal wooden tables that encourage long, relaxed brunches. Both Will and Charlotte grew up and met in Kent, but baker Will learned his craft in Edinburgh's artisan bakeries. Oast offers a wide range of breads, from sourdoughs to rye, yeasted loaves to sweet buns, which all sell out fast. The counter offers an enticing selection of pastries (cheesecake cookies and pumpkin-spiced buns are highlights), plus sandwiches to enjoy with a perfectly poured coffee from nearby Curve Coffee Roasters.

68 Northdown Rd, Cliftonville,
Margate CT9 2RL
oastmargate.co.uk

Dozen

Locally sourced and long-fermented breads

There is nothing better than moving to a neighbourhood and discovering a nearby artisan bakery. Those living near Norwich's Gloucester Street have hit the jackpot with Dozen, which specialises in naturally leavened bread and long-fermented pastries using raw cultured butter. They bake with organic flour and British-grown whole grains, which they mill themselves. For such a small bakery, the variety on offer is impressive: look out for the olive fougasse, speck and Isle of Mull cheese croissant and the seasonal custard buns (the fig leaf is particularly good). There is a small shop, so you can you can fill your cupboards with British cheese, meats and dairy. If you do choose to eat in, relax the trio of window seats and order a filter coffee or a super velvety Bare Bones hot chocolate.

107 Gloucester Street, Norwich NR2 2DY
instagram.com/dozen_bakery

Grain Culture

Bustling bakery and larder shop

The ancient city of Ely has a lot going for it – not only the site of a magnificent Norman cathedral and Oliver Cromwell's former house, it is also home to Grain Culture. The bakery supply many of the best independent businesses in the area, but the Bake Shop General Store is their beating heart. It is a bustling, charmingly cluttered space lined with bookshelves and full of mismatched furniture. For a relatively small shop, there is an impressive array of different spots to relax in with your breakfast, from tables among the natural wine racks to a quaint walled garden for sunny days. Focusing on the same core menu of classics since they opened in 2018, Grain Culture's pastries have been tried and tested to perfection, with their pillowy-soft pain Suisse normally the first to sell out. The larder shop is expansive, with a tasty selection that spans Neal's Yard cheese to Portuguese tinned fish and terrines, local honeys and unique bottles of natural wine.

Unit 16, Sedgeway Business Park,
Common Road, Ely CB6 2HY
bakeshopgeneralstore.com

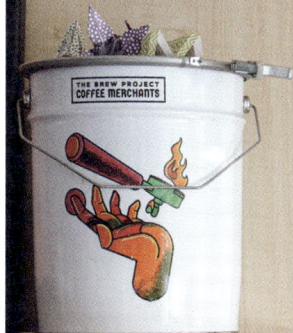

HOT DRINKS

THE BREW PROJECT COFFEE ROASTERS

ESPRESSO	£2.50
AMERICANO	£2.50

+ THE ESTATE DAIRY MILK / OATLY

FLAT WHITE	£3.00
LATTE	£3.50
CAPPUCCINO	£3.50
ICED COFFEE	£3.00

PUMP STREET CHOCOLATE

HOT CHOCOLATE	£3.95
MOCHA	£4.50

RARE TEA COMPANY

CUP	£2.50
TEA POT	£4.50

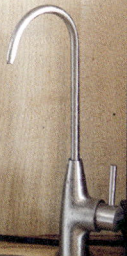

The Old Store

Multi-award-winning brunch spot

This popular brunch destination has a microbakery on site, so everything you eat is fresh out the oven. Their award-winning sourdough bread is very much at the heart of what they offer, with the all-day brunch menu highlighting this special staple, but The Old Store has scooped up award nominations and wins in everything from croissants to customer experience. There are drinks for every occasion, whether you fancy a locally roasted coffee, pear chai smoothie or even a glass of wine or a cocktail. Go all out and order the famed full-English (featuring a duck-fat hash brown) or try their sourdough pain au chocolat – a delicious twist on the familiar classic. The spacious cafe has a friendly feel, the walls decorated with owner Lewis King's striking landscape photographs and brightened with jolly, canary-yellow furniture. It's a great place to come with bigger groups, as there are plenty of large tables to lounge at.

5 Pedlars Mews, Snettisham PE31 7XQ
theoldstorenorfolk.co.uk

Gorse Bakery

French-style bakes with Cornish ingredients

Cornwall is best known for its traditional – and substantial – savoury pasties, but in recent years the county has welcomed a new wave of bakeries introducing a French style of delicate viennoisserie. The best of the bunch, Gorse is located among an unusual cluster of warehouse spaces in Lanteague studios on the north Cornish coast. Sandwiched between Petalon's whimsical, regenerative flowers and The Brew House's craft beer, this sparse industrial space is brought to life by families and friends chatting over their coveted breakfast treats. Gorse's interiors were created with a Cornish timber merchant and the food suppliers are equally local, with coffee and milk both sourced from nearby St Ives. Owners Nat Galliano-Hale and Anna Gerrans are often on hand to help you pick from the tempting array of pastries, and there is always something new, from apple pie Danishes to marmite and cheddar swirls.

7-8 Lanteague Studios, Scotland Road, Newquay TR4 9JG
Instagram.com/gorse_cornwall

Lilac Bakery

One-oven wonder

It is worth venturing to the outskirts of Exeter for the lovely Lilac Bakery. Owners Jenn Wickings and Eddie Goodwin took a bet on an empty betting shop in late 2021, transforming the venue into a charming artisan bakery. The operation is very small, with just one oven producing all the daily bakes from bread to buns, croissants to cookies. Jenn and Eddie are self-taught and between them they bake, barista, provide front of house service and wash up. They are busy but powered by passion, and their energy is evident in every detail of the homely cafe, pretty mismatched crockery and (most importantly) in the tasty bakes, which are made only with high-quality suppliers like Taw River Dairy for milk and Wildfarmed for flour. When it comes to deciding what to eat, the choice is overwhelming – the elaborate cruffins are always popular (flavours might include banoffee pie or ham and cheese), or visitors can opt for a classic pain au chocolat or brioche bun.

59 Cowick Street, St Thomas, Exeter EX4 1HR
instagram.com/lilacbakery.exeter

The Exploding Bakery

School friends' cake venture

The Exploding Bakery has been part of Exeter's high street since 2011, when school friends Oli and Tom took on a small shop with a rickety old oven and second-hand coffee machine. With a vision to provide the city's people and businesses with great cakes, they learnt on the job with some guidance from crash courses in baking and making coffee. Demand grew, and so did the Exploding team, eventually taking over the space next door in 2016 to expand the cafe and kitchen. It's now a comfortably roomy destination for a slice of galette (puff pastry filled with frangipane) and a cup of coffee, the tables big enough for a book, laptop or gaggle of friends. But if you can't get to Exeter, order a box of traybake cake or brownies to be posted through your letterbox.

1 & 2 The Crescent, Queen Street, Exeter EX4 3SB
explodingbakery.com

Farro

Unparalleled pastéis de nata

Farro is found on an unlikely but up-and-coming corner in Bristol's St Paul's district, right by the city's busy Bearpit roundabout. But the offbeat location doesn't deter devotees from arriving early at the weekend to pick up ultra-buttery kouign-amanns, dainty canelés and silky-rich pastéis de nata. Founded in 2015 by Bradley Tapp as a market stall and later moving into a small permanent home, this petite bakery is takeaway only, with just a couple of benches outside. But what it lacks in floorspace it more than makes up for in flavour: the team are serious about making truly excellent bread and viennoisserie. Their sourdough uses freshly milled grain from Gothelney the Farmer and T65 French bread flour from Wild-farmed, resulting in a distinct malty sweet flavour. If you are lucky, you might find croissant crisps on the counter: a thin slice of pain au chocolat, dipped in a mix of honey and cream, then baked until caramelised and crisp.

Facing onto Bond Street, 1 Brunswick Square,
St Paul's, Bristol BS2 8PE
instagram.com/farrobakery

WINE LIST

MANILLE DONNIOR   £19.50
*1 PINOT GRENACHE LANGUEDOC

*MAR. GRENACHE BLANC MARABELL

Both Manille Donnior wines reflect the
elements of the Roussillon mountain sea

RICO NUEVO   £16.95

small grangite production known for
making distinctive Grenache than old
bush vines on heritage soil

LENAZZA FRIULANO   £19.50

Mini Friuli, we have Italian wines
made with traditional methods

RETAIL PRICE LIST

EGGS - £3
COFFEE BUTTER - £7.50
ORANGE PICCALO - £7.50

HONEY - £8
JAM - £4.95
OLIVE OIL - £12

FIG PICKLE (TINS) - £9.50
MULTI OAT SAUCE - £6.95
OAK RUM -

KIMCHI MAYO - £6.50
JARDLINE - £8
CHILLI SAUCE - £6.50

CHICKPEA JAR - £8

BREAD ROLLS - £18.95
BUTTER ROLLS - £8

GRANKHOUSE COFFEE   250g   £5.50

FARRO   HOUSE COFFEE

FARRO   250g   £9.50

FARRO   HOUSE COFFEE   1KG   £53

Hart's Bakery

Tasty treats in the heart of Bristol

Hidden away in the Victorian arches under Bristol's Temple Meads station is an artisan bakery you won't want to miss. Conveniently placed for anyone arriving in Bristol by train, Hart's is the ideal start to a day in town. There's a bounty of breads, from golden loaves of sourdough to malted wheat and sunflower, as well as a viennoisserie section (made with specialist cultured butter from Estate Dairy) including quince and almond bostocks, dauphinoise Danishes and the classics. Hart's also serve appropriately *hearty* lunches, which can be anything from slow roast pork belly with blood orange som tam and pickled beansprouts to coronation chicken buns. The brainchild of Laura Hart, who started the bakery in 2012 when she was made redundant from her career as a pastry chef, everything here is made onsite in the open-plan space, kitted out with gleaming ovens and coffee machines.

Arch 35, Lower Approach Road,
Redcliffe, Bristol BS1 6QS
hartsbakery.co.uk

Landrace

Bakery, bistro and bar

So loved is Landrace that it's not unusual for customers to travel from outside of Bath to visit. Founded by Andrew Lowkes and his business partner Tom Calver (from nearby Westcombe Dairy) in 2019, the bakery is known for their unbeatable cinnamon and cardamom buns and their delicious sourdough bread, made from 100 per cent stoneground UK grains. But this is not just a bun shop. Above the bakery is a charming bistro and bar (fittingly monikered Upstairs at Landrace) where you can feast on plates of buttermilk fried partridge, Cornish crab and Jerusalem artichoke or a girolle tagliatelle buried in parmesan – and then mop up the sauces with a slice of Landrace sourdough. They don't open on Sundays, so if you're just here for the weekend then be sure to stop by on the Saturday.

61 Walcot Street, Bath BA1 5BN
landrace.co.uk

Sol Bakery & Cafe

Slice of Argentine sunshine in a former Little Chef

Only those in the know will turn off the A303 into Chicklade service station to visit what is possibly the most unusual speciality bakery in the UK. Sol is the creation of Argentinian-born Mili and Pepa, who met in a tiny Wiltshire village in 2020. They discovered a love of baking during lockdown and started making empanadas together, which they originally sold from their homes. The venture was amazingly successful, and in 2022 they took a leap of faith when the opportunity arose to take over the site of an old Little Chef. This simply decorated canteen-style cafe is a little slice of Argentine heaven, selling freshly made sourdough, irresistible focaccia sandwiches ('English classics with an Argie twist', like the Argie BLT), sweet treats and, of course, empanadas. The perfect artisan fuel to break up a long drive.

Chicklade Service Station, A303, SP3 5ST
solbakeryandcafe.uk

Rye Bakery

Heavenly bakes in a former church

Just off Frome's main street, in a glorious, lovingly restored former church, is Rye Bakery. Set up in 2017 by enthusiastic Frome locals Owen and Amy, Rye was born from a seriously foodie background: Owen spent over ten years honing his skills working with bakers around the world, specialising in viennoiserie and sourdough bread, and met Amy (who previously cooked at Owen's mum's cafe) through their shared love of food. After a run of pop-ups making pizzas at festivals and markets, the couple started Rye, showcasing their passion for local grains to make their celebrated sourdough. The space is grand but has a welcoming feel, bustling with kids or groups of friends eager to relax over a baked snack and a good cup of coffee. Everything on the Rye counter is utterly divine, from glossy croissants to dense chocolatey brownies – and the lunch menu will convince you to stay for your next meal, too.

Whittox Lane, Frome BA11 3BY
Other location: Station Approach
rye-bakery.com

COME UNTO M

RYE BAKERY

SPACE

smoking

RYE BAKERY

WELCOME

WE ARE OPEN TUESDAY
-SATURDAY 8:45-4PM

WE ARE SERVING
BREAKFAST, LUNCH
PASTRIES & COFFEE

OUTDOOR SEATING
AVAILABLE

Tŷ Melin Bakery

Goods baked with love

Owning, running and nurturing an artisan bakery is a true labour of love, requiring time and dedication – so it seems fitting that the entrepreneurs setting up these special places are often partners in life and business. Tŷ Melin is the creation of Lance Gardner and Angharad Conway, a couple who met through their shared love and experience of baking. A true family affair, 'tŷ melin' translates as 'Mill House' in Welsh – the name of Angharad's family home. With prestigious bakery experience between them, including at Hart's (p.160), Pavilion and Richard Bertinet, it's no surprise that Tŷ Melin's sourdough is perfectly bouncy and their viennoisserie expertly constructed. They are best known for their special 'croissant bomb', a trademarked pastry made from a crispy croissant shell with a range of fillings including sticky toffee pudding and apple compote, finished with a treacly glaze.

49 Wellfield Road, Cardiff CF24 3PA
Other locations: Bayscape, Usk Vale Park
tymelinbakery.com

House
Sourdough
£3·80

The Angel Bakery

The heart of Welsh artisan food

Abergavenny is a Welsh town known for its artisan food businesses and local creativity, and The Angel Bakery and general store is found at its heart. When it opened in 2016, two bakers (Sophie Kumar and Polly Hunter) made everything from long-fermented sourdough breads to immaculately laminated pastries. The team has grown, thanks to increased demand, and Angel also now supply wholesale customers. There is a lot of choice when it comes to choosing your breakfast here: fresh fruit Danishes are delightful (often showcasing a seasonal stone fruit like peaches or plums) and their satisfying, sugary brown butter and hazelnut cookies are perfect with a coffee. But it is the assortment of breads that define this bakery: opt for bouncy focaccia (which also feature in their hefty sandwiches) or one of their five organic sourdough loaves. Set within the bakery, the shop is a wonder emporium of artisan foods and produce, all sourced from like-minded, eco-conscious companies.

50 Cross Street, Abergavenny NP7 5EU

theangelbakery.com

Flori

Lisbon-inspired neighbourhood bakery

Flori may look unassuming, with its small footprint, plastic crates in place of chairs and giant bags of flour to perch on; its bakes are anything but. The breads and pastries here are seriously good and people will queue an hour around the block to get them. A proud neighbourhood bakery where regulars come for catch-ups with the team as well as coffee and croissants, Flori is owned by Lotte Rogers, who grew up baking with her nanna and affectionately named the bakery after her son. Not only do her team work with local farmers and millers to source ingredients, they also grow produce for seasonal fruit and custard Danishes on their own allotment (the strawberry custard crumble pastries are a thing of beauty). Lotte's first bakery job was in Lisbon, so it's no surprise that her cinnamon-dusted pastéis de nata are better than most you'll find in the UK.

9 Scarcroft Road, York YO23 1ND
instagram.com/flori.bakery

Northern Rye

Masters of slow fermenting

Northern Rye is off the beaten track, found by the river in Newcastle's creative Ouseburn district behind a discreet front on the corner of a red brick residential building – those lucky locals. Owner Robbie Livingstone opened the bakery in summer 2020, but his journey started years before when he gave up a more conventional career in printing to follow his dream. The breads and pastries here are made using slow-fermentation techniques, with the sourdough sometimes proving for up to 28 hours (which gives a deeper flavour while also aiding digestion). The almond croissants, generously loaded with nutty frangipane, always fly off the shelves at breakfast; for lunch, sample their brilliant bread in a sandwich heaving with tasty fillings such as Coronation Chickpea or New York Deli (stuffed with cured meats, salad, cheese and pickled onions). The spot is rightly popular with locals, but it would be unfair not to mention Northern Rye's more illustrious clientele – the bakery supplied Beyoncé and crew with croissants when she was touring nearby!

4 Riverside Walk, Byker,
Newcastle upon Tyne NE6 1LX
northern-rye.co.uk

Triangle Bakehouse

Gut-friendly breads

Triangle owners Aaron and Vic didn't start out as bakers. Aaron worked as a car mechanic, but a passion for home baking led him to a local bread workshop, and then a shop at The Handmade Bakery in Slaithwaite. When Vic was diagnosed with Crohn's, the couple set out to make wholesome, gut microbiome-friendly bread, and so Triangle was born (initially operating as a microbakery delivering bread as a subscription service from their cottage kitchen). Triangle specialises in traditional breads, religiously using heritage wheat and organic stoneground flour – some of which is even freshly milled in their bakery. Their signature sourdough – a mix of organic rye, spelt and einkorn – is a beautiful and nutritious loaf, but it's also worth trying some of the quirkier options, like cheddar and black pepper or the multi-seeded varieties.

Oldham Road, Ripponden, Sowerby Bridge HX6 4EH
trianglebakehouse.co.uk

Long Boi's Bakehouse

Colourful, creatively flavoured cakes

It's a neighbourhood affair at Long Boi's Bakehouse, where owner Jenny kneads heart and soul into every bake. Found on a residential street in Levenshulme, Long Boi's opened in 2020, taking over a corner shop site that had stood empty for sixteen years. Jenny honed her craft working at Mancunian bread royalty Pollen (p.190), but wanted her own space to be full of vibrant colour, moving away from the sparse Scandi look. There is a strong community and sustainability ethos here, with plenty of vegetarian bakes, and the amazing (all-women) team are always working on a new special. Popular bakes include their vegan blueberry and dark chocolate babkas and the picture-perfect lamingtons (vanilla genoise sponge filled with homemade jam, dipped in ganache, coconut and petals, topped with fresh whipped cream and finished with the Long Boi's signature morello cherry). Where else are creations drizzled in pink icing, covered in sprinkles and adorned with flowers? This is colourful, decadent baking at its best.

40 Forest Range, Manchester M19 2HP
longboisbakehouse.com

Nova

A feast for the eyes (and the mouth)

The shiny modern exterior of Nova in Leeds Dock couldn't be more unlike what you'll find inside – a bakery that prides itself on patient and intuitive techniques with an emphasis on championing nature and its most wholesome produce. Founded by sisters Sarah Lemanski and Hannah Mather in 2019, Nova is the only speciality bakery of its kind in Leeds. The bread here is all sourdough, made from organic stoneground grain. Because all their wheat comes from small-scale Yorkshire farmers, the grain is constantly changing with the seasons, an exciting challenge for the Nova team to navigate as they have to adapt the recipes as they go. The viennoisserie selection is small but excellent, and there is also a small shop selling homemade pantry provisions like jam, pulses and granola.

The Boulevard, Leeds Dock, Leeds LS10 1PZ
novabakehouse.com

Pollen

Manchester's minimalist bread temple

Like many indie bakeries, Pollen started out under unloved railway arches (in this case, by Manchester Piccadilly station) before graduating to a permanent home in the industrial area of Ancoats. Their flagship site is a delightful place to spend a morning, with extensive seating and light flooding in through the windows, but they have a second, smaller branch in the Kampus development as well. Pollen's loaves use naturally occurring yeasts and are slow-fermented over 28 hours, allowing a complex flavour to develop. The results are delicious – opt for something from their brunch menu to see for yourself (the signature Pollen Breakfast of white butter beans, Welsh leek sausage, smoked ham hock, oyster mushroom, charred tomato and fried egg on their 28-hour sourdough is especially good). When it comes to the sweet treats, the almond croissant (with a hint of citrus) is a bestseller for a reason, and the fluffy, cinnamon morning bun – made with a buttery, brioche base – is equally delectable.

Cotton Field Wharf, 8 New Union Street,
Manchester M4 6FQ
Other location: Kampus
pollenbakery.com

Companio

A true community cornerstone

Neil Large worked in the construction industry until the sudden passing of his brother inspired a career change and Baneta Yelda came to the UK as a refugee from Iraq and worked in the NHS, before deciding to retrain. They met at the School of Artisan Food, became friends, and the rest is history. The result of their joint imagination and hard work, as well as the investment of artisan food enthusiast Phil Pryor, Companio is a bakery with a clear community focus, where staff and customers chat like old friends. Just a minute's stroll from Pollen (p.190), this corner of Ancoats is a mecca for bakery connoisseurs, and Companio has built a devoted following for its focus on high-quality heritage grain breads and flavour-packed pastries. Choosing a standout item from the menu is impossible: the savoury brioches are unbeatable (the Turkish eggs variety is a must), and the more classic viennoisserie are also among the best.

35 Radium Street, Ancoats, Manchester M4 6AD
companiobakery.co.uk

Aran Bakery

Stylish bakery from star baker

If you are journeying to the Highlands, stop here en route. Found in the quaint town of Dunkeld, *Great British Bake Off* alum Flora Shedden is behind this beautiful business, with its whimsical floral entrance and chic, minimalist branding. 'Aran' is an old Gaelic word meaning 'bread of loaf', and the name is apt: with seeded rolls and cheddar and kimchi toasties, bread is at the centre of the offering. Flavour and style go hand-in-hand with everything Flora creates, from the loaves stacked high on the bakery counter to the Danishes adorning her social media feed (including praline or potato dauphinois). Aran is a feast for the eyes. There are a few places to perch inside, but better to grab your goodies and wander round the picturesque town.

2 Atholl Street, Dunkeld PH8 0AR
aran-bakery.com

ATHOLL STREET

ARAN BAKERY
SOURDOUGH
CAKES
PASTRIES
BUNS
COFFEE
LUNCH

Bostock

Dab hands at dough

Everything that comes out of these ovens is reliably delicious, from sourdough breads to precise, French-style viennoisserie. Named after a French pastry made with leftover bread and almonds, Bostock make the traditional kind along with more creative varieties (like banana and pecan). Pâtissier Ross Baxter (who co-owns the bakery with his wife Lindsay) trained with Michelin star chefs across the country (winning the Scottish Food Awards' Pâtissier of the Year in 2018), so it's no surprise that Bostock's bakes are brilliant. Dab hands at all things dough, they are known for their sourdough bread (made over 36 hours with organic flour) and bulky almond croissants, as well as the eponymous bostocks. The original bakery, a staple on the high street, can feel cramped at peak hours, but the newer East Linton branch is airier, popular with larger groups and cyclists cruising along the dramatic North Berwick coastline.

42 High Street, North Berwick EH39 4HQ
Other locations: East Linton
bostockbakery.co.uk

Bandit Bakery

Exceptional vegan bakery

Bandit Bakery deserves an award for creating exceptional baked treats without butter – this cult Aberdeen
bakery is entirely vegan. Established in 2021 by Pete and
Sarah Leonard, there is often a frenzy of fans queuing
outside and the goods sell out fast, bagels and bourbon-
laced canelés flying off the shelves like, well, hotcakes.
The friendly staff don't take themselves too seriously,
but they do care immensely about the quality of the
ingredients they are putting into their products (the breads
use the brilliant Scottish white and wholemeal bread flours
grown in East Lothian at Mungoswells). They are best
known for their famous cinnamon buns, particularly
tempting on a Friday when the all-day happy hour gets
you a coffee and bun for a fiver.

51h Rose Street, Aberdeen AB10 1UB
instagram.com/banditbakery

Two Eight Seven

Celebrating the craft of baking

A little bakery that makes a big impression, Two Eight Seven by Sam and Anna Luntley quietly excels in producing some of Scotland's best bakes. The duo were behind Bakery47, a self-described 'work in progress' hoping to 'increase people's care for the things they eat, drink, share and celebrate'. The couple closed Bakery47 in 2017, not because it had been a failure but because it had been too much of a success; rather than expand the business, they decided to move on and find a new outlet for their ideas. Opened in 2021, Two Eight Seven is just that: a small studio brimming with wildly imaginative things to eat (bramble and custard brioche, cavolo nero macaroni pie, chocolate and buckwheat lunar cookies iced according to the moon cycle), interesting produce from local suppliers and positive community spirit.

287 Langside Road, Govanhill, Glasgow G42 8XX

twoeightseven.co.uk

Kaf Coffee

Experts in everything from beans to bread

Kaf excel at everything they try their hand at. Originally known for their superior speciality coffee (hence the name), they are now also admired for their trolley of glistening laminated bakes, ranging in style and flavour from classic croissants to adventurous inventions (the Cubanos with ham, cheese, pickles and mustard is a must-try). The tiny royal-blue venue is found in the eclectic Partick area of Glasgow, and there is normally a queue out the door. Owner Leo Belcher and team produce an impressive supply of viennoisserie, cakes and sandwiches (don't miss the Buffalo chicken with cowboy caviar made with bean and tomato salsa), but this bakery also stocks a wide range of specialist food products to buy. Pick up unfiltered olive oil, artisan hot sauce, jars of beans, packets of gourmet crisps and, if you're feeling especially peckish, a pizza whipped up by the kitchen crew and packed into a mock-retro takeaway box, ready for reheating at home.

5 Hyndland Street, Partick, Glasgow G11 5QE
kafcoffee.co.uk

croissant

pain au choc

winter spiced bun

w/ warm spices, orange + saffron

cinnamon bun

w/ buttermilk glaze

almond croissant

babka

bos

Twelve Triangles

Ultra-sustainable slow baking

Founded by Rachel Morgan and Emily Cuddeford in 2011, there are now nine Twelve Triangles branches across the Scottish capital. They call themselves a 'scratch bakery', working entirely with cold- or slow-fermentation sourdoughs, with no additives and using only UK-grown and milled flour. Slowing the process down makes the bread more digestible and richer in flavour. It's not just the signature sourdough that's slow: even the croissants take four days to make from start to finish. Each branch has its own vibe, some operating as takeaway only while others offer seating – the Stockbridge cafe is the best place to head for a lazy breakfast (try the burnt honey custard, cardamom and apple bun). In 2017, Twelve Triangles launched their 'Kitchen Table' communal dining concept as a pop-up. Made into a permanent restaurant due to its success, it can now be found at the Easter Road location with a lunch menu celebrating beautiful ingredients and great suppliers.

9 Comely Bank Road, Edinburgh EH4 1DR
Other locations: Brunswick, Portobello, Duke Street,
Morningside, Easter Road, Melrose, Dalry
twelvetriangles.co.uk

Outlier

Hub of Glasgow's arty scene

Glasgow's food scene is electric, with an exciting roster of almost weekly new openings, from tapas bars to brunch outlets, Michelin-starred eateries to brilliant bakeries. Outlier already ticks a few of those boxes – an all-day dining spot for outrageously good brunch dishes with a talented team of bakers out back – and founder Steven Turner is not content to settle, with big plans to expand the space and future of the brand (an art gallery and farm are next on the agenda). The deliberately unfinished look (exposed brickwork paired with dark copper-hued tiles) and chatty buzz from the open kitchen gives the spot a laid back, creative feel. Sit at the counter, soak up the atmosphere and enjoy something from the bounty on offer, which might include anything from cardamom and custard sourdough buns; aubergine, sumac and preserved lemon focaccia; or soft maritozzi laden with whipped cream.

38 London Road, Glasgow G1 5NB
instagram.com/outlier.gla

Charred Apricot + Ricotta Toast
whipped ricotta, charred apricot,
smoked honey + fennel jam

Lannan Bakery

Immensely Instagrammable pastries

Lannan was an instant success when it opened in summer 2023, and their popularity has only *risen* since then. Every morning, before the doors open, fans form an orderly queue down the road in eager anticipation of their glossy maple and pecan plaits and bricks of custard slice topped with berry icing. Owner and Head Baker Darcie Maher's passion and creativity are evident in every detail of Lannan, from the beautifully designed shopfront to the bespoke handmade coffee cups. Especially impressive are the selection of bakes: recent highlights including a nduja, fermented honey and Murcia al Vino (goat's cheese) bun and a pain Suisse oozing with vanilla cream and chocolate chips that is almost too beautiful to eat. Devilishly photogenic, Lannan's offerings are something of an Instagram favourite, drawing many to make the pilgrimage to Stockbridge. It isn't unusual for the bakery to sell out within a few hours, so come early and be prepared to wait.

29-35 Hamilton Place, Edinburgh EH3 5BA
Instagram.com/lannanbakery

MILLY KENNY-RYDER

Milly Kenny-Ryder is a London-based travel writer and food photographer/stylist. She is the co-founder and writer of *Weekend Journals* and the editor of www.thoroughlymodernmilly.com. Follow her on Instagram (@millykr) to keep up with all the pastries she's eating (often with her two mini foodies in tow).

HOXTON MINI PRESS

Hoxton Mini Press is a small indie publisher based in east London. We make books with a dedication to good photography, passionate writing and lovely production. Should you wish to be considered for an updated edition, please send copious amounts of baked goods our way.